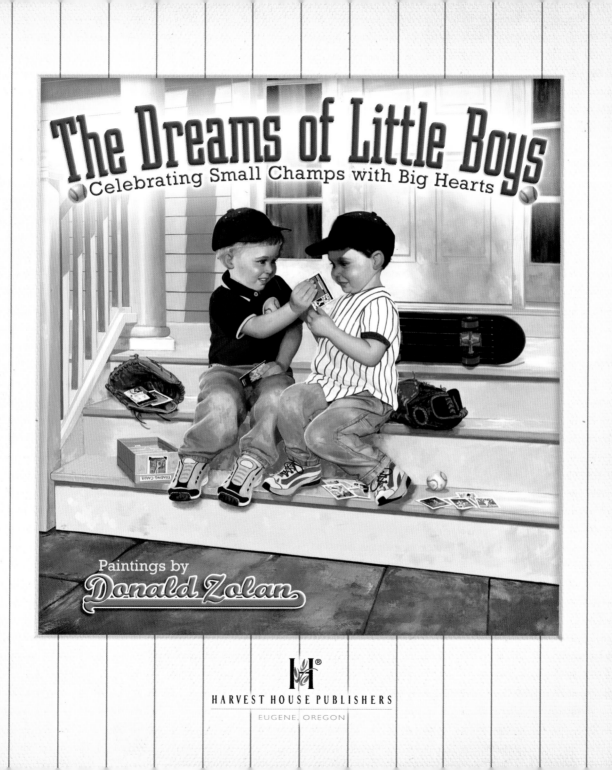

The Dreams of Little Boys

Celebrating Small Champs with Big Hearts

Paintings by
Donald Zolan

HARVEST HOUSE PUBLISHERS

EUGENE, OREGON

The Dreams of Little Boys

Text Copyright © 2005 by Harvest House Publishers
Eugene, Oregon 97402

ISBN-10: 0-7369-1473-0
ISBN-13: 978-0-7369-1473-4

> Zolan Fine Arts, LLC
> Attn: Jennifer Zolan
> 70 Blackman Road
> Ridgefield, CT 06877
> 203.431.1629
> www.zolan.com

Design and production by Garborg Design Works, Minneapolis, Minnesota

Harvest House Publishers has made every effort to trace the ownership of all poems and quotes. In the event of a question arising from the use of a poem or quote, we regret any error made and will be pleased to make the necessary correction in future editions of this book.

Printed in China

05 06 07 08 09 10 11 / IM / 10 9 8 7 6 5 4 3 2 1

One of the best things in the world is to be a boy; it requires no experience, but needs some practice to be a good one.

CHARLES DUDLEY WARNER

Playing football—using newspapers wrapped in wire and string—deep into the night on Reedsdale Street, under the light of the neon Clark candy sign. Sneaking into the North Side Harris Theater via the coal chute and being told by the manager, Mr. Lee, "I don't want you boys to ever darken these portals again." Being among the carload of boys Art Rooney would carry to Forbes Field in his 1948 Buick station wagon, where Steeler Bill Walsh taught Livingstone to snap punts...

BRIAN O'NEILL

There are many ways to become a winner. I think that it is more important to become a winner in life; then it is a lot easier to become a winner on the field.

TOM LANDRY

Just me and the ball. Running faster than I'd ever run. My spikes bit into the warning track and I put my right arm up. I drove my right foot into the padding and leveraged myself as high as I could go. My right hand grabbed the top of the fence and I pushed still higher as my left hand reached way over my head. My waist fell onto the fence top as I watched the ball land safely in the webbing of my glove. I balanced for a moment on the edge of the fence, then gently fell back to earth. The crowd's roar filled my ears…

AL JANSSEN
Let's Play Ball

Baseball is for the leisurely afternoons of summer and for the unchanging dreams.

ROGER KAHN

Once again a boy, on a drowsy summer afternoon, he lay in the shade of the orchard trees or, in the big barn, sought the mow of new mown hay, and, with half-closed eyes, slipped away from the world that droned and hummed and buzzed so lazily about him into another and better world of stirring adventure and brave deeds….he slipped away into the wonderland of dreams—not the irresponsible, sleeping, dreams—those do not count—but the dreams that come between waking and sleeping, wherein a boy dare do all the great deeds he ever read about and can be all the things that ever were put in books for boys to wish they were.

HAROLD BELL WRIGHT
Their Yesterdays

ndeed it is true that all life really begins in dreams…Surely mothers dream of the little ones that sleep under their hearts and fathers plan for their children before they hold them in their arms. Every work of man is first conceived in the worker's soul and wrought out first in his dreams. And the wondrous world itself, with its myriad forms of life, with its grandeur, its beauty and its loveliness; the stars and the heavenly bodies of light that crown the universe; the marching of the days from the Infinite to the Infinite; the procession of the years from Eternity to Eternity; all this, indeed, is but God's good dream. And the hope of immortality—of that better life that lies beyond the horizon of our years—what a vision is that— what a wondrous dream—given us by God to inspire, to guide, to comfort, to hold us true!

HAROLD BELL WRIGHT
Their Yesterdays

If you watch a game, it's fun. If you play it, it's recreation. If you work at it, it's golf.

BOB HOPE

When I was a boy we didn't have computers, Playstation, and all the fancy toys children have today. We played games like kick-the-can, hide-n-go-seek, ring-around-the-rosie, tag, hop scotch, and so on. Then there were things we did that had no names. We just made up the game and rules as we went along.

RON NEAL

Tennis and golf are best played, not watched.

ROGER KAHN

TOUCHDOWN

What you do in the off-season determines what you do in the regular season.

GEORGE ALLEN

The beauty of the game of football is that so often you are called upon to do something beyond your capabilities— and you do it.

DUB JONES

He has called on the best that was in us. There was no such thing as half-trying. Whether it was running a race or catching a football, competing in school—we were to try. And we were to try harder than anyone else. We might not be the best, and none of us were, but we were to make the effort to be the best.

ROBERT F. KENNEDY

The shed was one of my favorite places, full of mysterious tools, and drawers that were like treasure chests. It was where we kept our fishing gear, and where I would hide out and read my comics…

Every Sunday, when the weather was good and my dad didn't have chores, we would load up Granddad's old Ford Prefect with the split cane rods, a large thermos of tea, cheese sandwiches, folding chairs, and the morning newspapers. And the bait. The bait was either maggots or bread. I was fascinated by the maggots and loved to hold them in my hand and watch them wiggle their way in between the cracks at the bottom of my fingers. They had a cool, smooth tickling feel to them. Sometimes they'd get left in a rusty Old Holborn tobacco tin in the shed for a couple of weeks. If I lifted the tin to my ear, I could hear the buzzing of hatched bluebottles.

The river was a half-hour from our house. The roads were narrow with hedges and trees on either side. It was farm country. Lots of cows and oats and barley. Our bungalow backed onto a farm. It had a pond where I'd fish for newts with a worm tied to a piece of string.

PAT DONOGHUE

As a pastoral game, baseball attempts to close the gap between the players and the crowd. It creates the illusion, for instance, that with a lot a hard work, a little luck, and possibly some extra talent, the average spectator might well be playing; not watching. For most of us can do a few of the things that ball players can do: catch a pop-up, field a ground ball, and maybe get a hit once in a while....

MURRAY ROSS

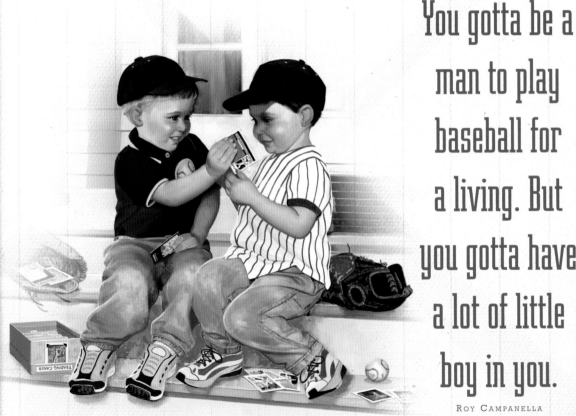

You gotta be a man to play baseball for a living. But you gotta have a lot of little boy in you.

ROY CAMPANELLA

17

Bang! a snowball from another quarter caught him fair in the neck.

"Here, you fools, you! Stop that!" cried Foxy, turning in the direction whence the snowball came and dodging round to the side of the store. But this was Hughie's point of attack, and soon Foxy found that the only place of refuge was inside, whither he fled, closing the door after him. Immediately the door became a target for the hidden foe.

Meantime, the Indian war was progressing, but now and again a settler would return to the fort for ammunition, and the moment he reached the door a volley of snowballs would catch him and hasten his entrance. Once in it was dangerous to come out.

By degrees Hughie augmented his besieging force from the more adventurous settlers and Indians, and placed them in the bush surrounding the door.

The war game was demoralized, but the new game proved so much more interesting that it was taken up with enthusiasm and prosecuted with vigor. It was rare sport. For the whole noon hour Hughie and his bombarding force kept Foxy and his friends in close confinement, from which they were relieved only by the ringing of the school bell, for at the sound of the bell Hughie and his men, having had their game, fled from Foxy's wrath to the shelter of the school.

RALPH CONNOR
Glengarry Schooldays

In the cooling dark of the August night the boy and his father sat comfortably on the veranda of the old Vermont farmhouse; though the younger was little more than a bulk of greater dark in the large shadow of the night, the older man's eyes rested gratefully on his son, as if thus all the tide of love might flow unseen from him to the boy.

EMERY POTTLE
"A Father and His Son"
Harper's, 1906

Two very superior bicycles went twinkling up the road to Plumfield one September afternoon, bearing two brown and dusty riders evidently returning from a successful run, for though their legs might be a trifle weary, their faces beamed as they surveyed the world from their lofty perches with the air of calm content all wheelmen wear after they have learned to ride; before that happy period anguish of mind and body is the chief expression of the manly countenance.

LOUISA MAY ALCOTT
Jo's Boys

Most unexpectedly, the boys did bring their friends and on the day appointed Mr. Seton found himself taken at his word by upwards of forty little white savages, as keen for fun as young America ever is. He told them they could go swimming in the lake if they wished. He led their sports, and that night, when they had thoroughly exhausted their animal spirits and were gathered about the campfire, he propounded his scheme. It was nothing less than organizing themselves into a band of play back woodsmen and seriously playing at woodcraft.

FRANK B. ARTHURS
"Boy Scouts Building for Manhood"
Outing Magazine, 1910

Been on my own since I was sixteen
Visions of flight filled my boyhood dreams
Superman was my hero, man made of steel
In my daydreams I joined him, it all seemed so real.

Fantasy flight
I always thought that I might
Childhood dreams can come true
It's all up to you.

FLOYD W. BLUE

A farm boy's life was rich with inventions and discoveries, and he was by no means a stranger to sports. He had his ball games in summer and his skates in winter. Work was adjusted so as to bring about friendly rivalry, as well as cooperation. Reaping, husking, building was done by "bees"; so called because they were busy and buzzing. The young folk ran races in planting and in digging. Life was full of fun.

AUTHOR UNKNOWN
"The New Country Boy"
The Independent, 1911

In baseball, home plate is where you begin your journey and also your destination. You venture out onto the bases, to first and second and third, always striving to return to the spot from which you began. There is danger on the base path—pick-offs, rundowns, force-outs, double plays—and safety only back at home. I am not saying, as a true fan would, that baseball is the key to life; rather, life is the key to baseball. We play or watch this game because it draws pictures of our desires.

SCOTT SANDERS

Boys, baseball is a game where you gotta have fun.

DAVE BRISTOL

Every boy grows up dreaming about playing in the NFL, and the greatest dream of all is to play in the Super Bowl. My boyhood dream was realized three times. I got a chance to suit up in Super Bowl XXIII, XXIV, and XXIX. The great thing about playing in the Super Bowl is that it is one of the few things that you dream about and then the dream comes true and the reality is better than the dream.

I think it's great to dream.

STEVE YOUNG

Timothy Winters comes to school
With eyes as wide as a football-pool,
Ears like bombs and teeth like splinters:
A blitz of a boy is Timothy Winters.

CHARLES CAUSLEY

It is in the pure open air of
heaven along that golf
works its wonders that make
it the joy of ardent youth.

ANDREW CARNEGIE

Golf is not just exercise; it is an adventure.

HAROLD SEGALL

His explanation for his passion for running is the stuff of all boyhood dreams.

"When I saw Haile running, I thought that perhaps one day I could be like him," Bekele told me before he went to Lausanne.

Unlike most boys with similar fantasies, Kenenisa never let go of his vision—but his ambitions to be an athlete did not chime with his parents' wishes.

"They didn't encourage me to become a runner," he said. "They wanted me to be a good student and then hoped I would become a professional—maybe a teacher or a doctor. They are happy now, because they've seen my picture on the television and read about me in the newspaper."

DAMIEN ZANE

Take pride in how far you have come; have faith in how far you can go.

AUTHOR UNKNOWN

The Win

So this one's for all the boyhood dreams, for kids who threw rubber balls against front steps and thought they'd play in Fenway Park someday.

This one is for old men and young boys, for drivers who listened to games on scratchy car radios. This one's for the people in New Hampshire and Vermont who listened on far-off stations because the local ones went to bed early.

You want to know what this means for Red Sox fans? It's everything, the only thing, the transformation of dread into dreams.

And me? I watched the playoff games with all the serenity of a squirrel staring down a lumber truck. My innards jittered. My brain rattled. I thought I heard the ceiling crack overhead, preparing for the roof to fall in.

You learn that mostly it's a wait-til-next-year kind of world. Nevertheless, I kept a place in my heart for one sport, one team, one boyhood dream, a token bit of foolishness.

It has come true, this dream, and it seems, after all these years, as pretty as a new bike.

Dan Mackie

On his first trip this boy took me fishing along a millrace in Maryland. It was a gentle stream whose size was in inverse ratio to the boy's expectations. Of course he had three hooks and of course he got them entangled in tree roots within a minute after they had touched the water. He pulled and at once guessed he had caught three whales.

LYNN ROBY MEEKINS
"A Boy Goes Fishing"
Outing Magazine, 1901

And so it went for my companions and myself on our recent fishing trip to Venice, La. Three days out on a boat owned by a friend, we encountered, brought aboard, cooled and eventually put on a grill the following: redfish, Spanish mackerel, flounder, speckle trout, pompano and sheepshead.

It was the stuff of boyhood dreams for someone who has always had a passion for fishing but little adult time to do it and maybe not the patience to watch a cork float above a bream hole for hours at a time.

JOHN FLEMING

Address to a Puck

Fair eh, your honest hockey place,
Great chieftain of the scarring face;
Between the boards with skates to lace:
    Your rubber froze,
Darting dangerous quick of pace,
    In slap shots rose.

The crackling ice on which you slide,
Chased by padded boys well applied;
In loss or victory you decide:
    Yours' not to let,
Where shots be accurate or wide,
    Streak towards the net.

Yes, your powers make cold winter fair;
In boyhood dreams young and old share,
With pride our true colours to wear:
    On Habs or Leafs stuck,
This O Canada's common prayer—
    Blessed be a puck!

DAVID MACLENNAN

You've got to believe deep in yourself that you're destined to do great things.

JOE PATERNO

It began at home on the couch, where they sat with tiny jerseys and big dreams. Eyes growing wide, staring past the pizza boxes and the potato chips. Watching every last minute of pre-game coverage, telling their dads to "Shhh!" Screaming "MOM, GET OUT OF THE WAY!" even though it was just 4:00 or 4:30 P.M. and the game was at least two hours away.

DAVE BUSCEMA

here rocks are scarce, duck-on-the-rock has become a game played with a baseball—roly-boly. The crowd's hats are lined up on one curb, and a boy with the baseball from the other tries to toss it into someone's hat. Whoever gets it so, runs to get the ball while the crowd scoots the other way. As he picks it up, he shouts, "Stand!" at which all must stop in their tracks, while the ball is hurled to "sting" any-one in sight; and the boy hit "rolls" for the next round.

ROBERT DUNN
"Games of the City Street"
Outing Magazine, 1904

Baseball, more than any other, is a generational game.

FRANK DEFORD

Every winter, he and his buddies would slide down the steep, snowy side of Monument Hill, just northwest of the Clark Building, on pieces of cardboard, or go to the top to skate on frozen tennis courts. Each summer, they'd play daredevil games on the daunting slope. "This was called 'Dead Man's Pass,'" he tells me, pointing up to a narrow ledge above the parking lot, explaining it was named for a drunk who took a bad fall. "The secret was running—don't take one step at a time."

Any kid who wanted to run with his crowd had to meet that challenge.

BRIAN O'NEILL

The distance to Long Lake was covered almost before Bert knew it. As the hockey game was not yet begun they spent half an hour in driving over the road that led around the lake.

Quite a crowd had gathered, some in sleighs and some on foot, and the surface of the lake was covered with skaters. When the hockey game started the crowd watched every move with interest.

It was a "hot" game, according to Bert, and when a clever play was made he applauded as loudly as the rest. When the game was at an end he was sorry to discover that it was after four o'clock.

LAURA LEE HOPE
The Bobbsey Twins

From the first time the ball is held, the first game ever played, the dream takes hold. For every young boy or girl who ever scampered around the bases and felt what it was like to touch home plate and be mobbed by teammates; for everyone who streaked across the outfield grass, thrust an arm out, opened their eyes and saw the ball was indeed in the glove...the dream has gripped them. It is the dream that one day they, too, might play this child's game as their vocation.

PASSION FOR THE GAME

This is a game for America, this baseball—a game for boys and for men.

Ernie Harwell

When I was a boy growing up in Kansas, a friend of mine and I went fishing, and as we sat there in the warmth of a summer afternoon we talked about what we wanted to do when we grew up. I told him I wanted to be a real major league baseball player, a genuine professional like Honus Wagner. My friend said he'd like to be president of the United States. Neither of us got our wish.

Dwight D. Eisenhower

If you can imagine it,
you can achieve it.
If you can dream it,
you can become it.

WILLIAM ARTHUR WARD